Moonsongs

Niyi Osundare

Spectrum Books Limited
Ibadan • Owerri • Kaduna • Lagos

Published by
Spectrum Books Limited
Sunshine House
1, Emmanuel Alayande Street
Oluyole Industrial Estate
PMB 5612
Ibadan, Nigeria

in association with
Safari Books (Export) Limited
Bel Royal House
Hilgrove Street
St. Helier, Jersey
Channel Islands, UK

© Niyi Osundare, 1988

First published 1988

Reprinted   2005

All rights reserved. This book is copyright and so no part of it may be reproduced, stored in a retrieval system or transmitted in any form or by any means, electronic, mechanical, electrostatic, magnetic tape, photocopying, recording or otherwise, without the express permission of the author who is the copyright owner.

ISBN: 978-246-017-6

CONTENTS

Phases I-XIV	1-26
Further Phases XV-XXIV	27
Moonechoes	47
Under the Mango Tree	49
When	51
Monday Morning	53
City Noon	54
Noonview	56
Nightfall	58
Out in the Night, Sleepwalking	59
Nightfire	61
Autumn Cantos	63
Feather in a Storm	66
Back to the Future	68
Shadows of Time	70

For

all who stood for
    life
when twilight thundered in
with a calvary of howling axes
and death suddenly sprang
from the armpit of waking stars

But Earth said No
to their crimson plot . . .

Noon yet, then,
at our forge of busy bellows

We shall break many
    moons
on the elbow of the river
deep, ever so deep,
like the rainbow of a thousand dreams.

Time is the robe
Time is the wardrobe
Time is the needle's intricate pattern
In the labyrinth of the garment

Phases . . .

The moon, too, is a dream . . .

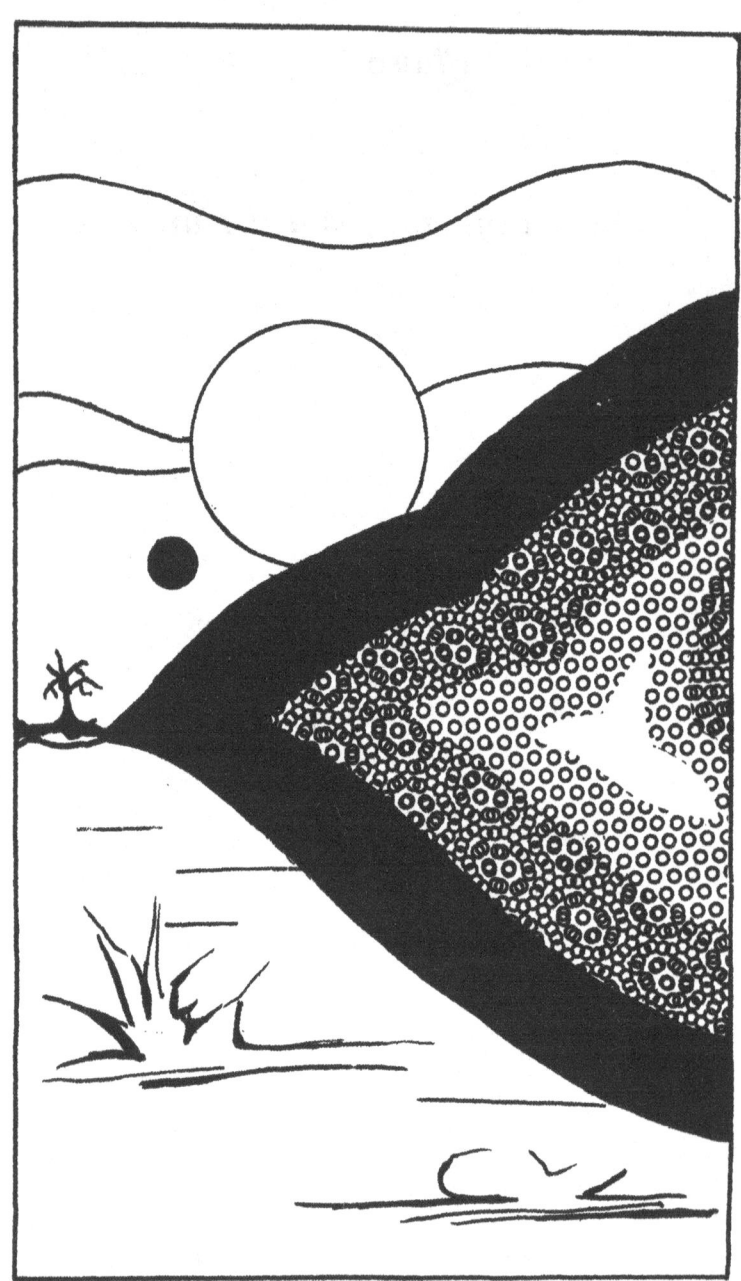

I

[To the accompaniment of lively *wọ́rọ̀* drumming, the following song, in call-and-response:]

> *Pèréẹ o pèré yojú l'ọ́run*
> *Àgbámùréré*
>
> *Pèréẹ o pèré yojú l'ọ́run*
> *Àgbámùréré*
>
> *Àṣèṣèyọ oṣù ó dà bí egbin*
> *Àgbámùréré*
>
> *Ká kọ́ṣu kóbì ká lọ mú ṣaya*
> *Àgbámùréré*
>
> *Ká tó dé bẹ̀ ó ti b'ọ́jọ́ lo*
> *Àgbámùréré*
>
> *Kírìjí kírìjí kírìjí pẹpẹlúpẹ*
> *Àgbámùréré*

Spread the sky like a generous mat
Tell dozing rivers to stir their tongues
Unhinge the hills
Unwind the winds
The moon and I will sing tonight

> *Kírìjì kírìjì kírìjì pẹpẹlúpẹ* . . .

Oh moon, matron, master, eternal maiden,
The bounce of your bosom
The miracle of your cheeks

Your smile which ripens the forests
Your frown which wrinkles the dusk
The youth of your age
The age of your youth
All, all await
The echoing thunder of my riddling chants

Kíríjí kíríjí kíríjí pępęlúpę . . .

Let the cricket slit night's silence
With the scalpel of its throat
Let nightbirds coo and cuddle
In the swinging Eden of their nests;
But when dawn finally climbs down
Through the leering rafters,
I will be a promise
Eternal like your seasonless sky

Kíríjí kíríjí kíríjí pępęlúpę . . .

And the moon masters the stars
Masters the sea
Sharpens every tip of its tidal teeth
Rattles every grain of its salty roost
Probes every drop of its diurnal blue
Ah! there are latitudes of sweat
On the brow of the sea;
A tropical truth taunts the waves
Surging beachwards like an armada
Of foaming sharks

Kíríjí kíríjí kíríjí pępęlúpę . . .

Bell-ringers, the shells shout time's segments
In the dormitory of dodging depths
Heard, not hearing,
Kneaded into millennial reefs and rocks
By the distant fingers of clever water
The penguin smells the moon

In the greying hem of its clumsy coat,
The beaches chew their sands
With the gritty vigour of rootless teeth

    Kírìjì kírìjì kírìjì pepelúpe . . .

New-sprung from the tabernacle of iron clouds,
The moon is a wandering sickle
Of gathering vows
With a dialect of whispers, covenant of simmering sighs:
The gallant plucks her like a fairy petal
On nights when the lanes are low
And flaming breaths tickle the ears of patient walls,
When moonmaids bathe lunar cycles in the blue mercy
Of scarlet waters
Their heads wavelocks of plaited bubbles;
Their wardrobe is mist,
Their sandals beadwork of fiery scales

    Kírìjì kírìjì kírìjì pẹpẹlúpẹ . . .

Fiery scales, fiery scales
So eloquent in the manhood of the sun

Oh sea

       season

            seasun . . .

The sun which blues the sea,
Which tones its flesh,
Before chasing twilight's orange
To the fringes of distant depths

    Kírìjì kírìjì kírìjì pẹpẹlúpẹ . . .

Beyond the palms, beyond the paddles
Beyond shimmering limits
Where the sea hugs the sky with a liquid passion,

The moon reads sunsteps inthe alphabet
Of protean sands,
The moon heals the scars of wounded winds

    Kírìjì kírìjì kírìjì pẹpẹlúpẹ . . .

Spread the sky
Unwind the wind
Let moonmares rein in the infinity
Of galloping hours.

Spread the sky
Unwind the wind
Let moonmirrors shape the amplitude
Of sundry strivings

    Pèré o pèré yojú lórun
    Àgbámùréré . . .

---

* Fresh, fresh does the moon appear in the sky
    Àgbámùréré

New moon is beautiful like a fairy
    Àgbámùréré

Bring yams, bring kolanuts, let's go and marry her
    Àgbámùréré

Before we get up there she has gone with Time
    Àgbámùréré

II

The moon is a mask dancing
              mask dancing
              mask dancing

The moon is a mask dancing

And in the milky grove
between the cloudmountains
the moon's tropical eyes
are chameleons of silver forests

The moon is a mask dancing

Her lips coiled
like corridors of a thousand snakes
breathing hot, breathing cold
lilting labial lyrics of tangled nights
Oh moon, mother me in the surging valley
of your knowing bosom:
there are clanging armours
in the aprons of the forest,
twilight clears a throat of bleeding spears,
      let dawn clip the tongue of murdering drums
      let dawn clip the tongue of murdering drums

The moon is a mask dancing

And in the tempered peace which rustles
the dew of nodding forests,
in the silence which fore-goes
the gallop of fertile thunders
let me see your voice
so lithe, so light, like eggs of starsparrows

I will not let fall the eggs
I will not let the eggs fall

The moon is a mask dancing

III

*I must be given words to refashion futures
like a healer's hand*
　　　　　Edward Kamau Brathwaite

We called the statue
To a talking feast
Before knowing the chisel
Never left a tongue in its rigid mouth . . .

　　From the silence of the seasons
　　From the hush which murdered the wind
　　With thunder's sword
　　We borrow the restless throat of *adoko*.
　　We borrow the permanent query
　　On the parrot's beclamoured beak

From the vowel of the river
From the consonant of striving valleys
We name the moon, we name the sun
We pledge a fluent chatter to the stammering sea

From seasons which pass but never part
I borrow moonbeams to shape the wind.

The *adoko* is a bird noted for incessant songs.

IV

[To the accompaniment of the song: *Òṣùpá o i
yuwá mi o, òsùpá o, i yẹ̀yìn mi . . .*]

Oh moon oh moon
Wife of the sun
Brother of the wind
Behold my front
Behold my back
Is my face still where it was
A little wink ago?

Behold my head
Behold my hair,
Behold my hair
So rugged now
Like the beard of a fallowing forest:
Can you see those grey serpents
Coursing through the shrub
With their fangs of flame?
Can you see these grizzling sprinkles
From the hearth of the sun?

Behold our garb
Behold our robe
Behold the generous hole
Which bares our backs for laughing winds
Behold the tired seams
Behold the absent buttons
Behold the threads which grin
Like missing teeth in the crotch of our trousers
But tell us, oh moon,
Was our wardrobe so weather-worn
When last you came our way?

Can you see the bamboo ribs
Of our walls strummed like a rusty harp
By the fingers of playful rains?
Can you count the furrows on the village brow
When the ploughshare has bared its teeth
And the season reaps the moan
Of broken worms?

Behold the dust
Behold the sand

    Behold the fickle echoes of the feet of stars

Behold the lake
Behold the river

    Behold the fugitive dance of sweating shoals

Behold the shade
Behold the sheen

    Behold the giddy rainbow of moving skies

Behold the leaf
Behold the nut

    Behold the merciless orgy of pampered grubs

How long now, oh moon,
The shifty twitch of the gossipy nose
How long
The iron I-brow of the foaming tyrant
How long now
The lengthening ivory of the youthful nail
How long
The hush in the house of the hoe?

Oh moon, oh moon
Wife of the sun

Brother of the wind
Behold our front
Behold our back
Is the world where it was
A little wink ago?

V

Frantic as a prentice poet
the young moon unfolds,
a wickless lamp
in the silence of lingering nights

trees preen their tops
walls unplug their ears
and hills advance,
minding every crater
on memory's road

moonrays have flared into song
the ballad sizzles in the chimney
of crooning noses;
stars red up the sky
with echoes of silver breaths

can it smell the echo, can it see the chant
a sky whose ears are sealed
by the wax of waning moons?

can it hear
when syllables thrum angry triggers
and consonants fall from heaven
like a hail of vengeful scorpions?

like a troubador
the moon unfolds her songs
by dusty roadsides of the sky;
the moon unfolds her songs
nomadic like a restless truth

VI

Night after night
the wind spreads out the sky

And the moon, too busy to sleep,
snatches fleeting dreams in tunnels
of nodding clouds,
swaying so solemnly to the summon
        of the drum
             of the drum
so loud now with the membrane of the sun

And with its rhythm of rocks
memory of meadows
hieroglyph of hills
with its ding-dong of dawn-and-dusk
the moon lilts and laughs,
a millennial tear standing hot
in the amplitude of its eye

The tear bursts into brook
ripens into river
then gallops like a liquid mare
towards the sea

All at dawn
when the moon is a seasoned navel
in the stomach of the sky.

VII

(in memory of Lake Nyos)

Waning waxing
waxing waning
the moon is the fiery rupture
of troubled depths:
thunder's midwife,
gallant of crimson storms

Ticking tantrum of sleeping earth,
the moon laughs in lava,
hauls molten spasm
from the spine of trembling fumes;
the moon, the moon's fingers
are epochs of ash,
her bowl lakes of lethal lore

Testicle of the giant clock,
each swing a seminal second
in the womb of scarlet winds,
the moon is the milky chime
in the ears of funeral seasons.

VIII

Moongrass is green like a first love
its blade whetted on stones
of whispering dew;
the rain pulls on its legs like a liquid yèpé,
then grabs the streets in showery embrace.
The pasture clears its tender throat,
and a jar of songs streams down
our milky ears

The reed has fluted the sage
fluted the season:
syllables lift their nouns
like eloquent rocks
and verbs pamper the wind
with transitive horns between their lips

Moonsongs have sealed the sky:
swaying nights murder the masks
which darken the dawn of groping limbs.

Have you seen gazing grains
in the winnowing window of lunar bowls?
Have you tasted the integrity of the seed
in the womb of grass?
hoeing seasons are owing moments,
and the moon pays its due
with the laughter of harvest raptures

* * *

Yepe are wide-mouthed loose-fitting Yoruba trousers which reach just below the knees

Moonsong is moonsweat
a greensome river trickling down the loins
of seeing skies:
daring dusts, building bridges,
unravelling the puffy crests of swaggering mountains

Moonsong is the truth
which cheers the wake of fleeing falsehoods,
the gem
which soothes the earth
when the chaff has taken its leave
in the fury of knowing winds.

Moongrass is moonsong,
the lofty depth of lilting valleys.

IX

Can you smell the footsteps of clouds
on the tracks of the moon
when flying winds cut a path
through a wilderness of leaves
and the stars depart with a bagg-
age of silent seasons across
their ancient shoulders?

Can you hear the sun stoking the fire
of the sky with its faggot of fancy
when a brazen furnace browns the leavened hump
of our skin, with ripenness's aroma
ever so green in the nostril of our noon?

Twilight, too, is day's cinder
when flowers fold petals in prayer
to passing mists, and the forest's ash-
en tongue sips honeys of brewing dew.

Oh hail of heels, rotor of wings
wandering rivers, nomadic oceans,
and seas of feet counting restless sands
on beaches of galloping waves

Oh trees which weigh their weeks
by the journal of fleeing birds
Oh body which reckons its hours
by the calendar of ticking breaths

Oh heels, oh trees!
and the plagues which christen the epochs,
the booms which branch the eras
the egret which chalks the roster

of passing moons
on slates of learned skies

How many hours will make a minute
How many oceans total one drop
Of elusive water
How many forests will make one tree
In regions of meticulous showers
How many . . .?

The clocksmith's fingers glow
With embers of punctual stars,
Scales of hurrying fishes,
Blushes of reluctant moons . . .
    and the whispering fear of flowing moments
    and teeming feet going coming
    on shores of rippling dials
    and solar beats reckoning the heart
    of time's patience
    and busy auricles divining the silence of waiting seasons.

Ah! the peacock cannot count
Her century of feathers,
The parrot cannot count the chimes
Which cat the bell of her restless beak.

X

Tell me, moon,
Where are your wrecks
Where are your wrinkles
Where, the creases left
On your wondrous robe
By the crow-foot fury
Of the wandering wind?

The tendril plies the seasons
And reaps the sponge,
The river's hot-browed swagger
In the empire of the mountain
Softens so slowly into the mellow commonwealth
Of the spreading coast;
The universe sows its minutes, reaps its hours:
Grey strands run their course on the bristling asphalt
Of cruising dreams.

Ashes are the echo of fire
The nose is the memory of the face
The drum is an open hint of a hide
That loved its flesh

The universe sows its minutes, reaps its hours.

And in those moments of joyous ripening
When green turns gold and gold melts
Into phantoms of wizened silver
Ticking mountains fine-ally strike their hour
And the world quakes with streaks of solar depths

Beyond the wilderness of stone
Beyond valleys of suffocating veils
Beyond Wednesdays of unpenitent ash
A Monday flings open the door of the week,
A pliant clay in its waking hand:
Supple moments, oh supple moments!
And brittle breaths unchain the dance
And ample hands unhush the drum
Not even the salt of the sea, so bitter
With foams of epileptic scars
Not even the deciduous hustle of declining herbs
Can grey this dappled dream
So gently planted in the temple of our sleep
The universe which sows its minutes
Will reap its hours

XI

And the moon dropped into our copper hands,
a murmuring melon with a lymph of throbbing dreams

succulent like a song, fresh like a fairy
coy, even to the fondling fingers of roving winds
and the rain which whets its lips
for the nipples of swinging gardens.

The moon is a green sap which learnt
its golden skin from the school of truant seasons

wizened now, and deliciously yellow
a lunar juice meanders down the delta of the chin

its mangrove beard just one fishy brush
in a roost of fertile roots.

From the lore of its loins, from the ticking shrub
in its fragrant armpit,

the clouds assail the knife which
unrobe the melon, unveil the dream.

Ah! those fat, beckoning thighs, red as a riot,
and the tongue which nods and nods

in the cave of the moistening mouth. A happy valley
endures between the melons of moony mountains

a happy valley which pastures the lambs of our loins,
the shepherding staff which parts the lips of tickling waters

XII

(for Joan Rayfield, tenderer of fertile cultures)

Moonfire too is deciduous;
its conifers weep their leaves
like yellow tears;

And in the dappled darings
of autumn
when yearning winds press lyrical lips
on the apple's demurring bosoms,
skyfields are sweaty tracks
for the garnerer's unwavering feet

There is a golden chatter
in the bowers of busy barns
the air leans low with the fragrance
of active ripening;
moonchildren plod skyways
with baskets of mellowed vows
and the stars are heavy pods
of jolly juice

And the seasons which stirred the sod
which hoed the humus
when moonfields were green elves
sprouting from a vibrant wilderness of lunar pores;
those seasons, where are they now,
this moment of delicious shadows?

        Işẹ́ lòṣùpá ńṣe lálẹ̀de ọ̀run, lálẹ̀de ọ̀run
        Işẹ́ lòṣùpá ńṣe . . .*

But good old Armstrong
in his weightless walk,
did he trample moonharvests
in the science of green visions?

Busy is the moon in the compound of the sky
Busy is the moon

XIII

Some say
you moon
are the
ash es
of the
sun bath
ing limpid
night in
the grey
ing of
your silence
pallio echo
of solar
thunder s
are you

XIV

Mooncantation

(Gong)

The moon the moon is the eye of the sky, the ear
of patient twilights, the udder of looming seasons;
the moon is the ticking thunder in the clock
of infinite clouds.

The moon the moon is the molar of the rain,
the ligaments of dust, the appetite of the dew;
the moon is the hourglass which wasps its
waist in the furnace of swinging seasons

The moon the moon is the femur of the mountain,
the loin of the valley, the womb of the lake;
the moon is the serpentine phallus of the road

The moon the moon is the gullet of the
swallow, the arson of the parrot's tail, the
roving universe of the eye of the owl; the moon
is the twitching bicep of the river

(Flute)

The moon the moon is the dungeon of the dollar,
the leaden accent of the pound, the yell of the yen;
the moon is trade by batter

The moon the moon is the cannibal stomach
of slaving galleons, Badagry Elmina Bagamoyo
Port cf (S)pain, the crayon claws of the
apartheid dragon; the moon is the Atlantic
babble of History

The moon the moon is the serenade of the storm,
the precocious scalpel of the waking grass,
the muddy murmur of faithful floods,
the moon is the hoeless famine of
leanward seasons.

The moon the moon is the whisper of the grave,
the puking pandemonium in the navel of
the marketplace, the lightning in the
antelope's savannah heels; the moon
is the tenacious shimmer in the snail's
millennial trek

(Gangan)

The moon the moon is the lymph of the lore,
the tail of the tribe, the AMEN of absent
prayers; the moon is the ram's last nod
in the vigilance of the ramadan

The moon the moon is the historian's *if,*
the philosopher's *ergo,* the rhymer's larynx;
the moon is the cadence of the leaf in
symphony of the forest

The moon the moon is the fable of stone,
the epic of iron, the syllable of wood;
the moon is the sparkling song on the lips
of retreating darkness

The moon the moon is a crown without a king,
the shoal without its sharks, the flame without
its fang; the moon is the throaty clatter of
breaking chains of breaking chains of breaking chains.

(Gong, flute, gangan, shekere and heavy drums . . .)

A *gangan* is a metal bell; A *shekere* is a calabash laced with cowries and used as a rattle

Further Phases

The dream, the dream, is a moon . . .

XV

[In the background throughout, a persistent sound of pestle in mortar, supplying a rhythm to the poem and the accompanying song]

>*Poro poro poro poro*
>*Òsùpá olomì rooro*
>*Tó bá dì ròlé á bésu lórí*

The moon pounds her yam
in the apron of the night
Time to sing time to sleep
Time for the supple-white grub of the sweating sky

>*Òsùpá olomì rooro*
>*Tó bá dì ròlé á bésu lórí*

Her pestle is *iroko*
Her mortar a cratered depth
In Oroole's bosom. The yam, when pounded,
Is the clay rump of Agidimo mountain

>*Òsùpá olomì rooro*
>*Tó bá dì ròlé á bésu lórí*

Her soup is the sea
With a teeming tribe of simmering fishes
Her spice is the loyal shrub
Which tickles the nose of lofty hills

>*Òsùpá olomì rooro*
>*Tó bá dì ròlé á bésu lórí*

The stars will eat
With their restless eyes
A galaxy of teeth
Awaits the steaming skies

> Òsùpá olomì rooro
> Tó bá dì ròlé á bé̩ṣú lori

Midnight feast, midnight fair;
When the deed is dawn
And the clouds spread out in drunken ease
You pick your teeth with showers of rain

> Òsùpá olomì rooro
> Tó bá dì ròlé á bé̩ṣú lórí

The moon pounds her yam
In the apron of the night
With a milky pestle
And a jar of easy joy

> Òsùpá olomì rooro
> Tó bá dì ròlé á bé̩ṣú lórí

Remember tonight, oh moon remember
Remember them who torture their beds
With a scorpion of ravaging hunger
In their lizard stomach

> Òsùpá olomì rooro
> Tó bá dì ròlé á bé̩ṣú lórí

Remember, oh moon, remember
Our house of hunger which savoured
Your sizzling pestle
Never tasted the busy silence of the afterstew

> Òsùpá olomì rooro
> Tó bá dì ròlé á bé̩ṣú lórí

Remember the lucky hand's ceaseless journey
To the market of the mouth
Remember the wounded thunder
Which stokes the blaze of empty hearths

>   Òsùpá olomí rooro
>   Tó bá dì rọ̀lẹ́ á bẹ́ṣú lórí
>   Poro poro poro poro . . .

---

* Moon of the liquid eyes
  When it is evening, you behead the yam

* Òrọ́ọ̀lẹ̀ is a spectacular inselberg in Ikere-Ekiti.
  Àgìdímọ̀ mountain is a towering hill in Ado-Ekiti on which Christ's School is situated.

XVI

Now I know why the caged bird sings
Why the caged bird sings
Why the caged bird sings
Now I know why the caged bird sings
When the Moon is a knot of strings

The slope of night finally loiters
through the convex cornea of the sky;
and silence rakes up the streets
with epaulettes of terror

Now I know why the caged bird sings

A kiwi-ed boot traps a star
in a regimented shimmer
the skybird flips and flaps
as a cagey night now turns
a galaxy of sweating feathers

Now I know why the caged bird sings

Why the caged bird sings
Why the caged bird sings
Why the caged bird chants every note
on the saddle of crawling hours
when swagger sticks twine into
blustering vipers in the trembling squares
of our gathering fears
patriarchs who plough the word
are snake-charmers now
in the streetcorner of our dreams

Now I know why the caged bird sings

The General missiles a swagger
and a nest of edicts jets out
of his adamantine mouth . . .
The general is up, up, up
The general is up
There is a beltful of scars
In the furrows of our sweating backs

> *Now I know why the caged bird sings*

Night
when·minutes goose-step
in barracks of golden eggs,
the barrel of the gun ever so smooth
with crudes of petroleum rackets

> *Now I know why the caged bird sings*

Why the caged bird sings
Why the caged bird sings
The night ticks on like a giant clock;
and the young moon eyes its infant watch:
Dawn will not be long
Dawn will not be long
Then shall we all know

> *Why the caged bird sings.*

XVII

The lion borrows it name
from the eloquence of its mane;
the forest's *oríkì*
is the green syllable
of towering trees.

And what dumb gold
when drought has mined the leaves
and the birds, voiceless vagrants,
drift, drift, north with their baggage of songs?

The world is a mask dancing
                mask dancing
                mask dancing
Every agile sole knows the sizzling symphony
of the winged dust.

There is a fleeting flock
in the pasture of the moon:
the shepherd senses his twilight
in the static mirror of the eye of the sheep

The rain fell in June
and December licked it brown
with its feline tongue:
they who marvel the sinews of our dust
let them ask what happened to the offsprings
of our yester-showers

The rain is going going going
like a long-besotted bride

Oriki is a praise name

But if the sun drags the river
into its scorching harem,
can it lift the sands
from the armpit of earth?

The world is a mask dancing

XVIII

The moon is an exile
in the territory of the sky
with a fugitive baggage
and platforms of rocky sandals

ex
   patri
      ated

by hostile fumes
and unrepentant poisons
of foreign factories

The moon flees the sea
with a mercury tear
in each eye:
the whales bemoan their flanks;
sands cannot manage
their pestilence of crabs

*

And from brimming banks
pampered barons telescope moonface
with glitters of looted quarries,
gaping monarchs tickle moonmaidens
with their noisy crowns
and pliant hacks ply skyroute
with scrolls of our ravished history . . .

Oh cycle of fugitive triumphs;
night peddles frantic eggs with missing yolk:
but dawn tends the bloom of breathing winds.

XIX

A madding moon
has sold the stars
sold the rocks
there is a bickering banter

in the budget of the sky.
The moon plundered the gold
drained the diamonds
and bartered its silvery ore

to the merchants of night
whose claws are cold
whose teeth are crowded tusks
of the ivory of our dreams

The moon has felled the forests
laundered the lakes
harassed the hills:
a yellowing chill stalks

the steps of lunar magnates.
The moon borrows a bullion from Mars
pawns hapless moonchildren to Jupiter;
and when skysages challenge

the dimness of the deeds
the moon pleads its sword,
pleads the bayonet tongue
of its eager guns

Now the moon has crowned our silence
gripped our songs
laid a frenzied ambush
for the syllable of our sooth

A madding moon
has sold the stars . . .
and when a wounded thunder
seeks the sanctity of the skies

Ah! the moon, the moon
will be one rotting pumpkin
in the fringes
of a smoking dawn.

XX

On moon oh moon where is your horse where, your haste
Who reaped your gallop in the furrows of the sky

Oh moon oh moon where is your wardrobe, where, your ward
Who spread your silk in the loom of the sun

Oh moon oh moon where is your hoe, where, your hatchet
Who farmed the yam in your silvery barn

Oh moon oh moon where is your udder, where, your pitcher
Who mothered the milk that bathes your limbs

Oh moon oh moon where is your bank, where, your boss
Who forged the coins in your beady eyes

Oh moon oh moon where is your sage, where, your song
Who carved the wood of your towering tree.

XXI

The moon is a mask dancing

She needs no spectacles to see our roofs
rust-tongued, fear-furrowed, squeaking now

like a baffled hen panting
after the hasty exit of the hawkish sun.

And the sages who argue without their teeth,
beside fireplaces gone cold from litanies of

crippling woe; our bones which creak and crack
in the funeral shadows of eating chiefs.

With its ears the moon sees the Soweto of our skin
and painfields so soggy with the sweat of a thousand seasons

The moon is a mask dancing

In Grenada where Sunset nurtures freedom
with bayonets and cackling cannon

In Managua where reddening flares
brave the breath of Twilight storms

In the sorrows of our South deep, so deep
like scars of millenial lesions

The moon is a mask dancing

But tell me, what is a tale without a head,
a face without a nose, a noun without a name

What will the sky ever be
without the earth of his wife?

What will the answer be
without its question?

The moon the moon is a mask dancing.

XXII

Ikoyi

> The moon here
> is a laundered lawn
> its grass the softness of infant fluff;
> silence grazes like a joyous lamb,
> doors romp on lazy hinges
> the ceiling is a sky
> weighted down by chandeliers
> of pampered stars

Ajegunle

> here the moon
> is a jungle,
> sad like a forgotten beard
> with tensioned climbers
> and undergrowths of cancerous fury:
> cobras of anger spit in every brook
> and nights are one long prowl
> of swindled leopards

The moon is a mask dancing . . .

Ikoyi and *Ajegunle* are areas in Lagos

XXIII

[Drums throbbing, a yell of happy voices]

The moon this night is an infinity of smiles
with a beckoning brow
and cheeks of dimpled joy.
A seasoned chuckle spreads out
her face like a glowing canvas;
her lips are honey,
her voice one roll of dappled echoes

The forest hugs those echoes
in the shimmer of twilight spells. Charmed,
leaves tremble with a lingering fire,
branches twitch their thighs,
winkless in their pampered zeal

The moon, this night, is the laughter of the lake,
one silver eye in a magnitude of ripples

> . . . Thin-bodied joy,
> Mirth of cackling drums
> Melody of forgotten rainbows
> Aroma of simmering dusks . . .

The moon, this night, is the balm
of weeping wounds,
healing glare in a bowl of fireflies.

(Drums becoming reluctant, the voices less assured)

The moon, this night, is a rugged master
Teregúngún màjà gúngún tere

With withering smiles and snarls of crimson echoes
Teregúngún màjà gúngún tere

His forehead is a universe of scorpions
Teregúngún màjà gúngún tere

His eyelashes a mesh of iron bars
Teregúngún màjà gúngún tere

He struts the clouds with a retinue of whips
Teregúngún màjà gúngún tere

His path a winding saga of bristling stones
Teregúngún màjà gúngún tere

His eggs are bigger than his hens
Teregúngún màjà gúngún tere

His water much harder than an ancient rock
Teregúngún màjà gúngún tere

The moon, this night, is taller than the sky.
Teregúngún màjà gúngún tere

Teregúngún màjà gúngún tere is a rhythmic refrain, it has no meaning; borrowed from a Yoruba folksong.

XXIV

*think of our eyes
sharing one sky*

— Joseph Bruchac: 'Awatawesu'

Gather your hems now
Unfurl your shadows
Tell your fairy feet the road is waiting
Time for that last dance across
The threshold of the swaying sky

    Softly softly
    Softly sways the masquerade of the seasons

Unflinching brow, you who once lit up
The temple of the sky,
Golden pumpkin now in the furnace of dawn,
You have kindled the comb of the cock
Lending rising eaves their mysty trumpet

    Softly softly
    Softly sways the masquerade of the seasons

Across silver continents
Across oceans of rippling dust
Beyond deciduous discs of winking groves
Beyond tall chronicles of whispering depths
Across silence, beyond the superstition of the sea

    Softly softly
    Softly sways the masquerade of the seasons

Across the gripping muse-ic of the waking grass
In the throbbing cadence of busy nests
From the ancient chamber of patient drums
Songs ripen the foetus of the day
A misty rhapsody clears the throat of yawning dawns

    Softly softly
    Softly sways the masquerade of the seasons

The palm tenderly pledges its wine
To the parting queen,
The lake throws up its favourite fish
The hill gently yields its eloquent echo
Trees wave their leaves like bewitching fans

    Softly softly
    Softly sways the masquerade of the seasons

Behold the blue distance of prancing mountains
Behold the mellow magic of romping clouds
Behold the fairy laughter of homing maidens
With baskets of stars, garlands of crispy suns
Behold the amplitude which teases the edge of beaming skies

    Softly softly
    Softly sways the masquerade of the seasons

Quiet now the fancy of the forge
Dew-drenched, the tongue of seminal fires
Quiet now the dialect of the adze
Mist-mobbed, the prattle of the hoe
Quiet, quiet the pod of stirring seeds

    Softly softly
    Softly sways the masquerade of the seasons.

Moonechoes

Shadows across the path

Under the Mango Tree

(for Afam, who once wrote something similar)

> . . . and so many lives hanging green
> on racks of ripening branches

The Easter sun has, finally,
translated December's flow
into marvels of milky green,
milky green, awaiting the fattening yellow
of basket seasons . . .

> *a hoary blast swells the throat*
> *of a distant horn*
> *a disobedient jazz boards*
> *the butterfly wings of the wind,*
> *settling glum on the sweaty ears*
> *of laden donkeys.*

The hanging tribe swings
from leaf to leaf
to the melody of sighing winds
to the orchestra of rocking twigs . . .

> *beside the stream which flaunts*
> *waters of doubtful springs*
> *under a tree so tall now*
> *it hardly knows its sprawling roots,*
> *revellers douse stiffening fires*
> *with petrols of boot-legged gins*

And the green clan ever so restless
in the boisterous cradle of the wind:

a capering birdling squats briefly
on the tree's parting turf,
where sunrays peep furtively
at the moistening soil
and the sky eavesdrops the rolling
whisper of sleeping leaves . . .

> *the mortal murmurs of musing mangoes,*
> *of crude climbers and missiles*
> *from starving quivers;*
> *and suddenly, each fruit a toll*
> *of expiring winds*
> *each toll a tale*
> *each tale a tail of coiling snakes*
> *ah! mangoes man goes. Man*

Goes in so many lives hanging green
on racks of ripening branches.

When

the sun's silver terror roars into a whisper
and shadows fall to earth,
with a dark pain in their airy joints

the clock's faithful hands limp over
its figured face, their fingers so light
with dusts of time's unalloyed gallop

life's river shrinks and swells
in the bewildering groin of intractable forests
where leaves rise and fall like salaaming elves

the teeth of the mountain are sour with the sun
and steaming valleys are bowls of flesh
with the flighty spice of ancient winds . . .

The bone heeds the summon of the flesh
with a femur of fevers, marrows of epochal depths;
zebra clouds untangle their digital winks,
and ticking vapours swell the tale of migrant oceans:

tales:
of the cane which traps the moons
in the bitter history of lengthening islands,
of the kola which splits the seasons
with the spear of crusty lobes
of the *elulu* which sews the seasons
with the needle of throaty chimes

Not a knell, oh not yet a knell
      a thousand rains cannot slay the fire of the parrot

Not a knell
    a thousand oceans cannot rival the indigo of *agbe*

Not a knell
    a thousand showers cannot rout the camwood of *aloko*

Not a knell, oh not yet a knell
    a thousand moths cannot quench the candle of the moon.

No, not yet a knell

We shall not go till we have eaten the elephant of the moon
We shall not go
till our scrupulous eyes have stitched the broken tendons
of the sky
We shall not go
till our green dreams spawn golden suns
in the chronicle of stubborn trees.

---

elulu is the time-keeper bird
agbe: deep-blue bird
aloko: bird with a deep-red colour

Monday Morning

(at Ibadan University)

staccato syntax
of metalled heels
confounding clamour
of sartorial colours
and
per..fumes loud-
er than waterfalls

Oh what frantic resurrection
after the festive golgotha
of passionate saturdays!
what painless awakening
after the red-light gethsemane
of crisbo gardens

and then
the dozing galilee
of lecture rooms
the seraphic snore
in library carrels . . .

monday morning
week's january
when doors slammed
on stubborn sins
await the sledge hammer
of dire fridays

Crisbo Gardens is a popular night club in Ibadan.

City Noon

at the height
    of the noon
        of a February day

sultry like every February day
and just as frenzied,

on the brow
    of the head
        of a sprawling city

throbbing like every other city
and just as frantic

the carrot seller bellows his wares
in the ears of hungry streets,
his tray one stubborn bunch of pink phalli
hard, seasonably hard,
a seminal wind rattles the hill's lazy beard
with a soft insistent query:
    behold the carrot
    but where, the stick?

where is the stick, where is the stick?

the stick is the fishseller's knife
(brutal in its finny shortness)
its muddy handle, its scaly blade
its brimmy howl of crowded water
paddling sharks, paddling shells
the stick is the broken moment
of the hook's tenacious anger
the stick, the

stick is the onion clamour
from the *moinmoin* temple
the dogged fire under the forbearing pot;
the stick is the tasty treat
which worsts the foppish pap
sparing its wardrobe of leaves

the stick is the canvas of the rainbow
here where gold is black
where the wind is red
where, where unbridled terror
hoofs moonmarble in cavalries
or crimson dusts

> the dollar, the dollar
> spits a purple swagger
> our vassal crowns lick its plague
> in yellow awe

February has come
also come is the sun's ultra*violent* rays
in the tropical chapter
of our riddled cravings

from its pubic dream
to its public din
the city lies like a slumbered bull
its carrot hard between its horns.

---

moinmoin is a steamed bean cake

Noonview

the laughing sun
    unties

the knot of quibbling birds
in their feathery parliament
below the trees . . .

    a fiery edict has sealed
    the larynx of the lyre
    And the forest leaps into green lores
    of song and rage:
    "Truth banners, truth banners,
    should they ever bear
    the banner of truth?"

*

Ruthless as a jealous artist
a raging wind wrinkles up
the garment of the forest
    every line a furrow
    on a grudging brow,
    every vein a streak
    of sneaky oaths

*

. . . and memory which breaks
the teeth of the grave . . .
    what happens to the snail
    which left its shell
    in the lengthy crevice of an absent rock?
    what hint, the mouth

which lost its tongue
in the labyrinth of the throat?

Ah! the giant stands in the rid-
dling sun
but cannot see his musing shadow

Cannot see his shadow
cannot see his shadow
rippling like a molten puzzle
in the grey truth of lengthening dusks

*

And boasts the drunken tyrant:
    "My chains are iron
     My walls are stone
     My breath is the raging fire
     Of skydragons . . ."

But death came,
not like a pounding giant
with legs of mortar,
not like a swaggering mountain
with a crown of dizzy clouds.
Death came
in the sneaky column
of meticulous rains,
in the yellow whisper
of the wind

Death came
in the stammering murmur of thunder

And . . .

Nightfall

Night one
finally stroke
abolished of
the inky
day dark
with ness with

A lone in barracks
star beheld of fireflies
the edict and lanes
    of truant thunders

The moon has pitchering mercy milk
gone down-sky for beggar children

Out in the Night, Sleepwalking

Was it a shrilling mosquito
that put the final scalpel
to the thin thread of sleep
drenching my swollen eyes in the innocent blood
of assassinated dream?

Was it . . .?

The window shut its latticed eye on a gazing night
the door stared eyelessly
then stepped aside, silent as sentry.
Through latch and lock, through yawn and yarn
I staggered into the heated embrace of fireflies
the hibiscus snoring furiously in its compost bed

The path, puffed like a mamba,
rose to my heaving breast
the trees having lost their head to the night
not even a learned moon entered rayful plea
for an earth convicted of inky crime
the bat pleaded guilty in its gymnastic sleep

Silence.
Silent as sleeping horn
Silence
Simple as clay
Save the hem and haw of a stammering toad
Save the whimper of lizards living loving
in wall fissures

And then came the Mermaid of Night
wading through the sea of darkness
her head a tangled foliage of cobras
Just one hiss
and there I was
committed back to sleep and dream.

Nightfire

I smell burning tracks in the nose of the night
the hills so red and raw in robes of fire

The night has killed the candle, lamed the lamp:
a triumphal flame rules the sky in garlands of gold,

Diadems of simpering ashes. Yes, night flaunts
its crown of crimson, snaking down the nape

Of *Oke Agidimo* where seasons are tinder
when the harmattan hurls its torch of needling grey

The night is dancing dancing dancing on stilts
of trumpeting stalks . . .

No symphony now from the shy brook which lost
its tongue to the dusty ambush of wayward drought

The night is dancing dancing dancing and the moon
drops a tear from her smoky socket. The night is

Dancing, the hill looming so hot, a smouldering giant
with gaits of glee

Winking gold in the iris of a gaping throng
whose roots whose grains sweat so feverishly

In the orbit of a widening pyre . . . . pouring buckets
of prayers from the lake

Of their labouring hearts. Let day break
let the day break so these swarming cinders

May tread into smokeless antimony in the eyes
of the sand. Let day break let the day break so

Dawn's ancient fingers may calm this angry ingot
in the furnace of the night

The night is dancing dancing dancing,
murmuring masquerade, vermilion, in shrouds of shadows

Ah! the night has gone on fire. Is anyone still asking
what became of the beard of the hill?

---

* the *Agidimo hill* on which Christ's School, Ado-Ekiti, is situated.

Autumn Cantos

I

October-red,
leaves break into fiery dance
on the blackening platform
of patient twigs
swaying, swaying to the breaking breath
of marching winds

II

forest streets
throb with golden gaits,
footfalls of accentuating bugles,
of homing veins in wreaths of amber
and blades tongueing leaves
like bayonets of

III

anger Of the anger of the rain
so swollen, so swelling, snaky streamlets
puff into adders of flood
copper-skinned in trenches of scales,
surging coastwards in boots of sand,
in medals of liquid silver

IV

fall-frilled,
the October moon is an aluminium bowl
on the fire of the sun,
her teeth slightly stained with plums of mirth
her face reddening now from
flames of the forest

V

yes, the moon, too,
ripening,
has savoured the sickle of the season
the swarthy accent of the reaper's hand,
the chocolate touch
of gathering skies.

VI

for, the apple is the song
of the fall,
of parting virtues
and vices deliciously moist;
a curious thrust between the hills
knowing waters in the cave of the seasons

VII

seasons. seasons. of sturdy stalks
gradually softening, then buckling
like a head-surrendering neck
but tell me,
the beauty of autumn,
is it wisely gold or youngly yellow?

VIII

fallen petals, petals falling
with lucifers of leaves
flaming mat
of mellowed blossoms
blushing every vein in vermilion smiles
oh fluent fancy of falling feet

IX

but who says yellow is
is the colour of the fall?
a shy green rides treetops
like a stubborn memory;
maples shake their heads,
knowing full well their gold is

X

grey. Oh the poetry of it all!
stanzas of scarlet, rhymes in red
the squirrel departs, a metaphor of nuts,
the wind one line in the lyric of the sun;
a raging fire quickens the river of the moon,
October-red.

Feather in a Storm

The storm has seized the sky
seized the sky like a long-awaited despot;
henpecked several seasons
by the moon's diurnal fingers,
a feather sails the brow
of howling spirals:

Fluffy tango in twangs of eyeful twirls
bouncing ballerina scribbling common lores
with tips of frantic toes:
a tilt
    a twist
        a raging trot
of frenzied veins,
the feather shrinks with every frown,
spreads out with the reddening flush
of giggling eyes

The hurrycane harvests a shadow
of sullen sugar
rattled roots and oceans
of capsizing branches;
a hawk telescopes the range
from the tower of clever clouds;
divining orphan chicks
and offals of assassinated henhood . . .

Old storms new storms
whirls of undulating wells

        old storms new storms
        and quivering quills in plagues of iron edicts

Old storms new storms
and fountains dense with labouring dreams

> Old storms new storms
> and skies young with hieroglyphs of coming pasts

*

And the feather scrawls grating graffiti
on the wall of the storm
with the styli of sooth
kandahah of capering wisdoms
And the sky reads the script
through its tear of rain
And a learned thunder fires the clay
of every letter
Only twilight is too dim to read—
between the lines

pounded plumes. Furied fluffs
the feather floats in the storm
of our seasons
with a spine of steel,
blade of monumental

Tongues.
The feather floats the storm
of our seasons
honing elemental whisper
into bellows of shaping thunders.

Back to the Future

Unborn dinosaurs   Energy of blazing ashes
fossil of coming moons   flame of foetal fires

And the sky coils up
like a wounded foil
with silver scars
and a universe of serrated passions;
an orphaned sun stands, squint-eyed,
on the trembling edge of a-mazing maps,
with a latitude of lashes,
planet of drowsy stars

>   Maps maps maps . . .
>   for the map is a promise of the compass,
>   bleedless veins and art-
>   eries of absent rivers
>   the map, the map
>   is history's whisper
>   in the ears of yester-morrows

The sun chases the moon chases the sun
in lofty depths and shadows of thickening fancies

>   Ah shadows!
>   falling back like robes of airy emperors,
>   falling forth like pythons of skyjungles

Shadows
of the inky belly of the pen:
nibs of eyes, sagas of spurting spirits
Shadows
of the Thesaurus ever so lush
with pastures of quickening words:

twilight suckles like a blank baby
and dawn flees the cradle,
its head mellow with grey fire

Echoes . . .
Time's chamber is a wilderness of echoes,
of distant hills and cavalry of looming caves
Echoes
In tomorrow's ear a drum
which woos the ardour of forgotten sticks.

Echoes . . .

Shadows of Time

(Anniversary of a future remembered)

The clouds drift by,
nimble puppies with eyes of marble:
the sun dissolves in the hands of journeying winds
then hardens into balls of ticking stone

>   I heard moonsteps in the corridors of seasons
>   The sky is aflame with dusts of hurrying dials

Night melts into day melts into night
and the sun, caught between two twilights,
essays moving shadows of dew and dawn;
beyond rigid longitudes of uneven chimes
beyond alien meridians of patterned crossings
the sun bares its clocky face:
its seconds of stars, its speedy hands
playing minute pranks with pendulums of History . . .

>   I heard moonsteps in the corridors of seasons
>   The sky is aflame with dusts of hurrying dials

For Time, too, has its latitudes:
the dripping rags of tumbling comets,
the lateral slit of the prompting drum
the restless spring of the heels of the egret
cruising home to hearths of chalky depths.
Ah! Time's latitude
is the petulant green of the tendril
the golden pepuce of the pawpaw
the crimson song of the bleeding grave

      I heard moonsteps in the corridors of seasons
      The sky is aflame with dusts of hurrying dials

Memory's minions all:
trees reckoning rings on the ripening finger
of mating forests,
the insolent grey in the jungle of the sage's beard,
the okro which, counting days, springs steel fibres
against the conquering knife,
those frantic dreams left in pawprints
of leonine mountains, awaiting
the levelling showers of angry clouds

      I heard moonsteps in the corridors of seasons
      The sky is aflame with dusts of hurrying dials

The harmattan looks back
    and sees the rain
the rain looks forward
    and smells the egret
Life's tides crash and crest
in the oceans of our growing eyes,
fling their fangs at the banks of our dodging dreams,
then slither seawards, a rippling python.
The tides, those tides, will come again
when the moon of our noon is crescent
above the roofs
they will come again
when the sun of our night
is hearth for our tropical strivings

      I heard moonsteps in the corridors of seasons
      The sky is aflame with dusts of hurrying dials

Time's door leans
on hinges of uncertain shores,
oiled by sooth,
dimpled by knuckles
of accumulated visions.

Keyholes here are dioramas
of purple thrones
guessed now from rusty maces
and excavated grandeurs of grey edicts.

    Time
    Time never runs its race
    Like a straight, uncluttered road
    Ah Time never does
    In Time's street are treacherous bows
    And friendly bends,
    Crucibles of "Crucify him!",
    Alleys of Allelujahs;
    The chameleon joins eyes
    With owls of luminous nights
    But the forest still cannot see the bird
    On tomorrow's tree . . .

Time is the robe
Time is the wardrobe
Time is the needle's intricate pattern
In the labyrinth of the garment
Time is the lingering aroma
Of a long forgotten dish

    Time the seasons
    Season the times;
    The forest sprouts, blooms
    And rots into seed
    The seed mothers the mountain
    The mountain mothers the river
    And the river springs green flowers
    In Edens of unsinning apples

        I heard moonsteps in the corridors of seasons
        The sky is aflame with dusts of hurrying dials

Deciduous,
then, the smile of the moon

deciduous
the leafy fire on the brows of the sun
Time masters our steps like a general
with a thousand stars,
drills our manifold musings like a grindstone
with a thousand teeth;
we fret, we fight, we pacify mortality
with busts of stone,
monuments of loudest steel;
but the rains capture rusty chinks
in the shield of steel
storms soften stony prides into
flakes of weathered dust;
wrinkles buried so fashionably by
centuries of rosy talcum
embarrass the face after one wink
of hasty sweating . . . But

Evergreen,
Time lives in other dreams,
evergreen:
the song of the busy adze
the breath of the forge
the unfettering energy of the word,
minds touching minds touching matter

a strand of grey left in the twilight wind,
a favourite dish, a characteristic smile,
the world catches the fragrance
of our flowering visions
blooming petals of everlasting gardens

Evergreen
their breaths, who stoke the flames
of our flickering fancies

Evergreen
their winds, who lace silent echoes
with rattles of fertile thunders

Evergreen
> ever green

> I heard moonsteps in the corridors of seasons
> The sky is aflame with dusts of hurrying dials

---

* Dedicated to the 70th anniversary of *West Africa*, the London-based news magazine in which the poem also made its first appearance.

www.ingramcontent.com/pod-product-compliance
Lightning Source LLC
Chambersburg PA
CBHW011746220426
43667CB00019B/2921